# Coping on Your Journey

## From Maladaptive to Resilience

Kelly Strand

Copyright © 2023 Kelly Strand

All rights reserved.

ISBN: 9798854201896

All of the photos in this book are my own and used with permission from the person in the photo, where applicable.  The poetry is from my original collection.

# DEDICATION

I would like to dedicate this book to my brother Andrew. He is 12 years younger than me and my only brother. He became a victim of, and was stuck in the bowels of our dysfunctional family. He was forced to cope with some extreme things, and take on more responsibility than he deserved in his childhood.

I remember taking him out shopping and having him over to my place for sleepovers. We had such a good time, and I am grateful that I was able to provide him some time away from home where he could relax and have fun.

We have lived in different states most of our lives, but he moved to Arizona about 10 years ago, and lived with me while he was saving money to buy a house. It was really nice getting to know him as an adult, and see him on a day to day basis. We had regular dinner dates, and I watched him settle in and start to build a new life here.

Despite his childhood trauma, he has been able to cope and make a better life for himself. Even though he has highs and lows as we all do, and sometimes struggles to find balance, he knows the importance of being able to cope. He finds and uses the resources necessary, he has a strong desire to heal, and he is resilient.

He is very smart, has a kind heart, is an amazing Cat Dad, loves Debbie Harry and Star Trek, and has an amazing smile.

I'm blessed to be his sister and have him in my life.

## CONTENTS

Introduction
1 Coping
2 Dysfunctional Roles
3 Shame
4 Emotional Maturity
5 Attachment
6 Impossible = I'm Possible
7 New Strategies
8 Find Your Container
9 Resilience
10 Closing

# INTRODUCTION

In follow up to my first two books, this book is a continuation of my journey to recovery and healing.

Healing is a life long journey. A journey full of learning, discovery, and finding your best self. Your best self and your whole self.

You have most likely experienced more emotions than you know what to do with. You may have understood some of them, and others may have been so painful that you stuffed them away.

Growing up with dysfunction, coping was something that we did to survive. But now that we survived our childhood we have a choice to change. The choice is ours, and it is possible to unlearn some of the behaviors we've had for so long.

By sharing my insights on unhealthy coping and those uncomfortable emotions, its my intention to show you new strategies and tell you that it is possible to adapt and change and claim the life that is waiting for you.

~ Kelly

Coping On Your Journey

# 1 COPING

**Coping. Definition**: an individual's effort to deal with, regulate and attempt to overcome problems and difficulties and reduce stressors

Coping is not a "bad" word, but it can become a dysfunctional crutch, whether we realize it or not. Some of our coping strategies may be deep rooted in our childhood, and have grown from our need to survive any way we knew how.

It is important to pay attention to how we respond to stressful situations and events in order to understand whether our coping strategies are functional (healthy) or dysfunctional (maladaptive).

**Maladaptive** coping. This refers to coping strategies or behaviors that are ineffective, harmful, or counter productive in dealing with stress, difficult situations or events. This probably sounds familiar and you may even realize that some of your coping strategies are maladaptive.

There is nothing to be ashamed of if you do realize that your coping strategies are not on the healthy side. Recognition is the first step. Once you recognize what your strategies are, you can make the choice and commit to learning healthy ways to cope.

There are a few different types of coping:
- **Emotions focused** coping: managing your emotional response to a situation instead of trying to solve the problem itself
- **Problem focused** coping: addressing the problem in an effort to eliminate the stressor
- **Avoidance** coping: an effort (unconscious or conscious) to avoid dealing with a stressor in order to protect oneself

Let's look at each of those a little closer and some of the healthy and dysfunctional techniques that are used with each of them.

**Emotions focused coping.** With emotions focused coping, we try to alter our own emotional state rather than try to solve the stressful problem.
- **Healthy**:
    - Mentally processing the event. Being able to understand with clarity what happened during and after the stressful event.
    - Taking time out for reflection. Intentionally taking the time after the stressful situation to fully reflect on what happened.
    - Relaxation and breathing. Recognizing that you need to relax and focus on your breathing during or in response to the stressful situation.
- **Dysfunctional**:
    - Going into denial. Denying or ignoring the stressful situation, or refusing to accept the reality of it.
    - Distancing or detachment. Disengaging or disconnecting from other's emotions in order to react calmly to situations.
    - Wishful thinking. Escaping from reality and forming beliefs about the stressful situation that are pleasing.
    - Worry. A hyper vigilant or obsessive strategy that seeks to learn, rehearse and/or anticipate a stressful event.

**Avoidance** coping is a behavioral response, often to excessive fear or anxiety, in which we avoid the stressor. This type of coping is very often related to childhood trauma and dysfunction and PTSD.

Avoidance can be categorized as:
- **Self protective** avoidance includes:
    - Withdrawal/retreat/isolation. Being anti social, believing other's won't understand, or struggling to connect with others.
    - Dissociation. Feeling detached from your body, the people around you or your environment.
    - Emotional numbing. Feeling empty or dead inside, or not caring about anything and being disconnected.
    - Silence. Pushing your emotions and feelings down. Keeping the peace at any cost.
    - Repression. The unconscious blocking of unpleasant emotions, memories, problems or stressful events from your conscious mind.
- **Directed at self** avoidance includes:
    - Self blame. This is often a survival response to childhood trauma. A learned behaviour that can lead to toxic shame.
    - Self destructive behaviour. This involves doing something that can cause emotional or physical self harm and most times the risk/consequences are not thought about.
    - Substance abuse or other addictive behaviors.

> This involves using or abusing substances, food, sex, shopping, or other risky activities in an effort to cope with stressors.

- **Directed at others** avoidance includes:
  - Acting out. This is a defense mechanism in which, by acting out, someone is able to avoid difficult feelings and emotions.
  - Narcissistic. Narcissistic people have insecure attachment styles and in order to avoid their own unhappy feelings they focus on controlling the emotions of other people.

**Problem focused coping.** With problem focused coping we have the intention of altering our external environment or our relationship with it.
- Cognitive problem solving
  - Identifying and analyzing the problem before responding
  - Deciding the situation is unchangeable
  - Coming up with different solutions
  - Making a plan of action
  - Resolving the conflict
- Behavioral problem solving
  - Seeking support
  - Seeking information

**Do you recognize these coping strategies?** Are you ready to change some of your maladaptive behaviors?

"Two words will help you cope when you run low on hope: accept and trust." - **Charles R. Swindoll**

"Peace is not the absence of conflict but the ability to cope with it." - **Unknown**

"Don't let your coping mechanism become your comfort zone." - **Unknown**

## Broken (Original poetry by Kelly Strand)

Like an hourglass
Never to be turned
An ever yearning
To be restored

Forging on  day to day
Engaging my time
Commanding my thoughts
To stay preoccupied

Scarcely managing to be
Outwardly strong
Struggling to safeguard
My broken heart

Building the walls
Locking everyone out
Creates a makeshift
Sense of comfort

Broken once
I gambled and lost
Cut like a knife
Never again

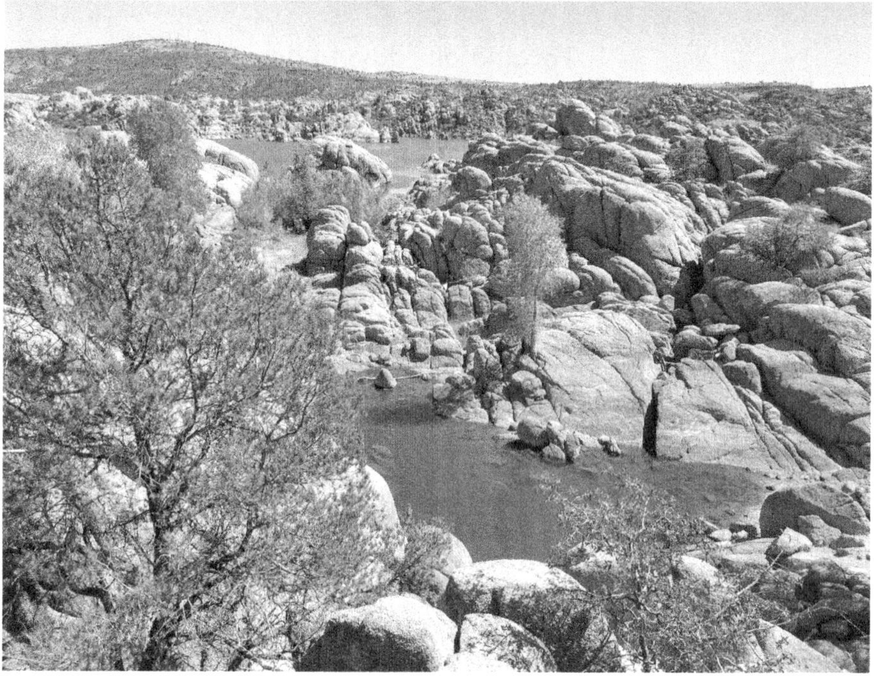

## 2 DYSFUNCTIONAL ROLES

Growing up in a dysfunctional family, there are several different roles that are assumed by the members of the family. Many of us don't even realize that we assume these particular roles, especially when we are young. Each of these roles have unique characteristics, and because of the dysfunction, the roles look different on the outside than they do on the inside.

For children, those characteristics will follow you into adulthood and cause you to carry on the dysfunction unless you choose to break free from the cycle.

The most common dysfunctional roles are:

- **Scapegoat/Black Sheep**: An outlier, or one who is different and misunderstood. Often times they are the most honest one in the family. They may be rebellious, impulsive or angry and they are never good enough. This one is cast aside and often blamed for problems that have nothing to do with them, and the family projects all of their unwanted negative traits onto the Scapegoat. Underneath the rough exterior the Scapegoat is often highly sensitive, emotionally intense or hyper empathetic.

- **Caretaker/Enabler.** The person who maintains the look of normalcy, supporting and affirming the unhealthy behavior. They may have a co-dependent relationship with the addict. They fuel the addict's unhealthy habits and try to keep them happy, even though they may be on the receiving end of verbal and/or physical abuse by the addict. In adulthood they continue trying to fix others and have an overall strong sense of responsibility and ownership of the problems of others.

- **Parentified Child.** The one who takes on the role of the other spouse in the absence of a healthy caretaker, and assumes adult responsibilities. The responsibilities they assume can be physical, mental or emotional. In adulthood they are frequently drawn to relationships with dysfunction and emotionally unavailable partners and they struggle with boundaries.

- **Mascot.** This one diffuses conflict in the family with skilled humor and other methods of deflection. They draw attention towards themselves and away from others where it could become volatile. They struggle to identify and express their own feelings for fear of causing conflict, so they mask them with a smile or a joke. They often never seem to grow up, and the family may foster their immaturity by protecting them from reality. On the inside, the Mascot is lonely, confused, insecure and full of fear, sadness and pain.

- **Lost Child.** The one just trying to survive and go unnoticed. They avoid personal interactions with the family, spend a lot of time alone, and repress their emotions. In adulthood they will struggle with interpersonal skills and maintain the feeling of being lost and unseen, often with low self esteem.

- **Golden Child/Hero.** This is the one who can do no wrong and proves their family is ok. They are terrified of being rejected or abused if they make a mistake. In adulthood they are drawn to achievement and success, are prone to perfectionism, and can become obsessively attached to others because they get their value and worth from external sources. Often they battle anxiety and depression.

- **Addict or Dependent.** This is the one who is the families reason for having problems. Often with addiction problems of their own.

**Do these roles sound familiar?** Which role do you relate to?

For me, I was the parentified child. I had not heard of this term until my therapist brought it up in one of my counseling sessions. Once I learned of the term I could completely relate to it. I assumed many of the duties as caregiver for my youngest siblings, as well as assumed responsibilities that my Mother would have normally done. Later in adulthood, I found myself in more than one relationship with emotionally unavailable partners.

In spite of the dysfunctional family roles we may be filling, in any situation we can can choose to do one of two things:

- Display victim mentality:
    - **Ignore** - ignore the situation and our emotional responses
    - **Resist** - resist the need to analyze our behavioral responses in order to try and improve
    - **Deny** - deny that there is anything wrong with the situation or event

- **Blame** - blame other people or situations for our feelings
- **Rationalize** - try to rationalize the situation and accept it as normal

- Display accountable behavior
  - **Forgive** - forgive the other person, or ourself for the part we played in the event
  - **Accept** - accept the behavior or actions as reality
  - **Learn** - learn from the situation and understand what is happening and why
  - **Self examine** - examine our emotions and responses to the situation
  - **Take action** - change the way we respond to our emotions when the situation occurs

Regardless of what role you may have assumed during your childhood, you can begin to release those familiar characteristics as you commit to and focus on adopting more accountable behavior.

"Some people play victims of crimes they committed." - OurMindfulLife.com

"Every family is dysfunctional whether you want to admit it or not. " - **Shailene Woodley**

"People who come from dysfunctional families are not destined for a dysfunctional life." - **Bo Bennett**

## Inner Child (Original poetry by Kelly Strand)

Sometimes
she wants to scream
let go of the pain
and forget

Sometimes
she wants to hear
the unspoken words
I'm sorry

Sometimes
she seeks answers to irrational questions
and wants to understand the lingering
confusion

Sometimes
she wants to run
from the fear
and hide

Sometimes
she listens
to the other
voice inside

Always
she closes her eyes
and regains
herself

Coping On Your Journey

# SHAME

**Shame. Definition:** a painful feeling of embarrassment or humiliation or distress caused by the consciousness of wrong or foolish behavior.

Almost everyone experiences shame at some point or another during our lives, and it is part of normal childhood development and socialization. Shame is a social negative emotion, and we often try to hide the things we feel ashamed of. Even though shame is a negative emotion, it is normal to feel mild shame.

Core (or Toxic) shame, on the other hand, disrupts emotional regulation and the development of a secure sense of oneself in relation to others.

**Toxic shame** is a debilitating feeling of worthlessness and self loathing. Toxic shame is normally rooted in childhood as a result of abuse, neglect or other traumatic experiences that make you feel like you are not good enough. People living with toxic shame may have:

- Ongoing feelings of inadequacy
- Constant negative inner dialogue
- Negatively impacted sense of self
- Thoughts that "I am a bad person" instead of "I did a bad thing"

There are several **causes of shame**, some of which are:

- Childhood trauma or neglect
- Mental disorders
- Being a victim of bullying
- Not living up to overly high standards that you set for yourself
- Feeling as though your flaws will be revealed
- Expectations not being met or experiencing failure
- Rejection from others

Shame is not guilt but they are often confused. Guilt is about something you have done such as making a mistake, doing something you know you shouldn't, or causing harm to another person.

**Guilt** = something you did wrong

**Shame** = something about you is unacceptable

Shame can cause a negative impact in your life and some of the effects may be devastating. A few of the negative impacts of shame include:

- Feeling flawed
- Social withdrawal
- Addictions (e.g. alcohol, drugs, sex)
- Defensiveness
- Bullying
- Narcissistic personality
- Physical health problems
- Depression or sadness
- Lowered self esteem
- Feeling empty or lonely
- Trust issues
- Compulsive or excessive behaviors

Shame is an incredibly difficult and uncomfortable emotion and because we want to get rid of it as soon as possible, it can lead to actions and choices that provide temporary relief. The temporary relief bypasses the immediate emotional experience but does not address the underlying issue. Some of those actions are:

- **Distraction** - provides temporary relief from self critical thoughts and emotions
- **External validation** - relying on external things or people in order to boost self esteem or ego
- **Secret keeping** - an intense urge to hide or conceal the insecurities that are exposed
- **Comparative analysis** - keeps self worth conditional upon who else is around
- **Self criticism** - negative or judgmental thoughts

As mentioned before, mild shame is healthy and toxic shame is unhealthy. Each of these have their own cycle which is as follows:

A **healthy cycle of shame** looks like this:
1. Incident occurs
2. Stress
3. Act out
4. Shame
5. Try to correct behavior

An **unhealthy cycle of shame** looks like this:
1. Trigger / preoccupation
2. Rituals

3. Act out / compulsion
4. Numbing / Self medicating
5. Shame

No one is born knowing shame, it is learned, and sometimes it is multigenerational. Until you understand the causes of your shame, and unless you address them, you will remain in an unhealthy cycle of shame. If you find yourself with an unhealthy cycle of shame there is help, and you can break the cycle.

Here are some small steps that can be taken:

- **Recognize the feelings**. Recognize the feelings, and that they are valid. Eventually they will feel normal.
- **Ask for forgiveness.** Start working on forgiving yourself. Make amends and ask others for forgiveness.
- **Let go**. Let the shame of your past go. Recognize the things you cannot change. Acknowledge that shame has no power over your life anymore.
- **Get help**. There is no shame in asking for help. It takes courage, and working through all the issues where shame shows up might take a long time. Healing starts by asking for help.

"Shame is a soul eating emotion." - **C.G. Jung**

"Shame cannot survive being spoken. It cannot survive empathy." - **Brene Brown**

"The truth releases us from shame." - **Lori Gottlieb**

"Shame is always easier to handle if you have someone to share it with." - **Craig Thompson**

"We are only as sick as the secrets we keep." - **Alcoholics Anonymous (AA)**

## Theoretically Alone (Original poetry by Kelly Strand)

Bitterly alone
Or is it all in my head
Confusing, persuading, eluding
From what otherwise isn't said

Alway wandering
Aimlessly at best
Am I destiny's pawn
In a shameless game of chess

Repeatedly questioning
For answers not known
For what have I been sent
To seek all alone

Sheltered by discontent
Sharing not my secret
Ever hanging on to the comfort
Of continuous discontent

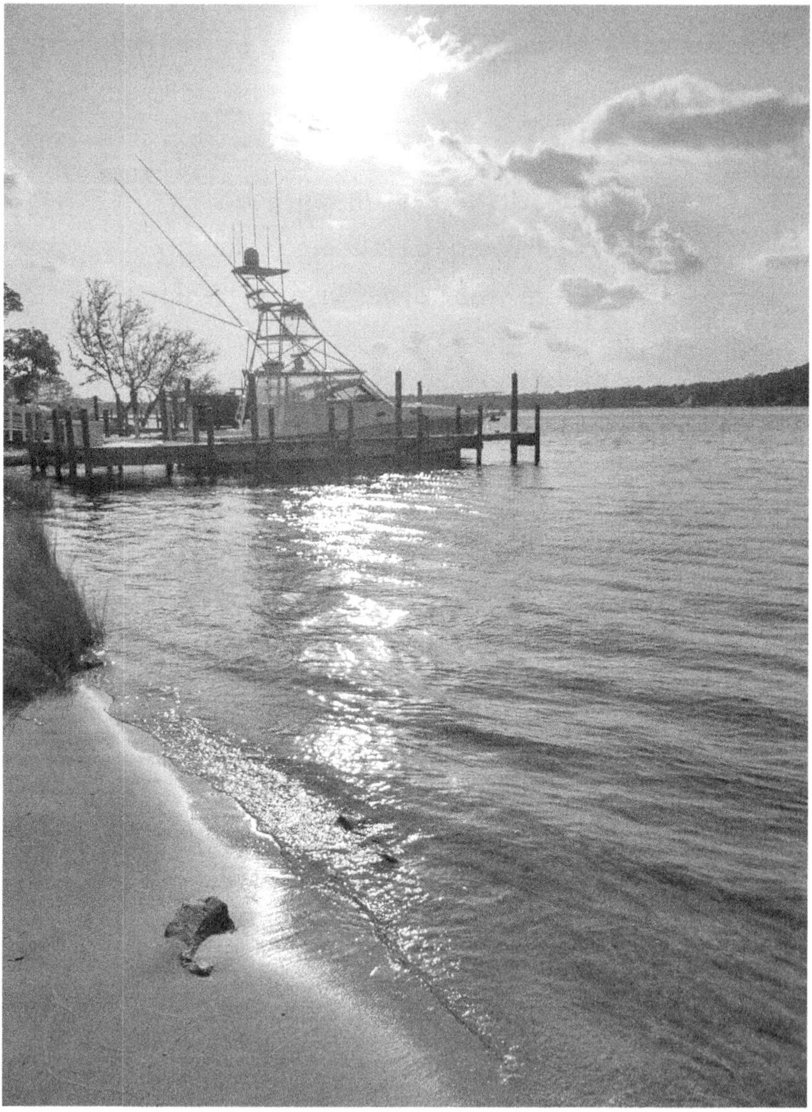

## EMOTIONAL MATURITY

Love and fear are the two root emotions. Every other emotion stems from those two emotions. Doesn't that makes emotions seems so simple? They're definitely more complex than that, but if you can assign your emotions to either love or fear, you'll start to see what your fear based emotions are, in order to address the underlying fear.

It takes a lot of practice, will power, and desire to master our emotions. Mastering our emotions does not mean controlling our emotions, I means we must have emotional maturity.

**Emotional maturity** is having access to, and control over, our emotional energies and allowing them to be an enrichment to our lives instead of a detriment. Our emotions give us an opportunity to optimally enjoy life's events.

Emotional maturity includes:

- **being self aware** - knowing your emotions, recognizing a feeling as it is happing
- **motivating ourselves** - commanding emotions to pay attention, delay gratification and stifle impulse
- **feeling empathy** - understanding others and recognizing their emotions
- **handling relationships (emotional intelligence)**- building and maintaining relationships

I've come across the phrase **"My emotions are not me, but mine"** several times, and it is a powerful statement. To me, this means that my emotions do not define who I am, but I am responsible and accountable for how I process and react to my emotions.

There are no good or bad emotions, just good or bad reactions. This is also a powerful statement. Learning to accept our emotions, just as they are is a sign of emotional maturity. And after you learn how to accept your emotions you will begin to be able to master how you react to your emotions.

Emotions are messengers of inner wisdom within us. They manifest physically and provide information about what we are experiencing and what we need to do. We all have inner wisdom. You've heard it before; that little voice inside of you. Or you've felt it; your intuition. **How do you deal with your inner wisdom?**

Feelings are our subjective expression of our emotions. They are how we perceive our emotions and assign meaning to the emotional experience. Feelings are influenced by our past experiences, memories, and beliefs. It is sometimes very hard to escape the influences of our past experiences or memories. And, if you have experienced trauma or grew up in in a dysfunctional family then there is another layer added to those influences.

**How are you feeling?** Today? In general? Are you unsure of why you are feeling a certain way? Understanding the emotions behind our feelings is part of being emotionally mature. Remember, there are no good or bad emotions, just good or bad reactions (feelings).

Maybe you have difficulty expressing your feelings. This is very often related to growing up in a dysfunctional family. Growing up with family dysfunction, we do not talk about things, or acknowledge our feelings so we are subjected to a negative emotion/feeling cycle, which we take into adulthood and often have a difficult and painful time trying to break free from.

I had been emotionally numb for so many years but I finally made the commitment to myself that I would heal my inner child. I wanted to understand my emotions and feelings. I wanted to be able to recognize them, not stuff them or react impulsively. I needed to build an emotionally healthy relationship with myself so I could then build healthy relationships with others in my life. During my therapy, I was able to do the work necessary to heal my inner child.

Before my inner child was healed, I had unregulated emotional energy. I had a childlike relationship with my emotions, which consisted of emotional flooding and numbing. Now, I am emotionally available and I have regulated emotional energy. For the first time in my life, I can say that I welcome all of my emotions and the feelings that result from them.

**How emotionally mature are you**? There is not a right or wrong answer, there is only room for growth.

"Emotional maturity allows us to accept all of our emotions, even the uglier ones we don't want to admit we harbor." - **Dr Nicole Lepera**

"Emotional maturity is taking responsibility for your own emotions. No one can do that for you." - **Rebekka Lien**

"When awareness is brought to an emotion, power is brought to your life." - **Tara Meyer Robson**

## Control (Original poetry by Kelly Strand)

Struggling at times
fighting me fears
insecurity biting
resulting in tears

Am I alone
or just lonely feeling
content with myself
time to start healing

No more haunting
close the door on the past
only I hold the key
this time is the last

Sometimes
Its ok to let go
And let emotions
Good or bad, flow

Questions and why's
Keeping safe my heart
Rediscovering me
A brand new start

Coping On Your Journey

# 5 ATTACHMENT

**Attachment. Definition**: a state of being personally attached; a strong emotional bond an infant (or person) forms with a caregiver, especially when viewed as the basis for normal emotional and social development.

Psychiatrist and psychoanalyst John Bowlby formulated Attachment Theory, which is a psychological, evolutionary and ethological theory concerning relationships between humans. The most important tenet is that young children need to develop a relationship with at least one primary caregiver for normal social and emotional development.

So much can be said about the importance of this theory. During early childhood the need for a relationship with a caregiver is instinctive, and the core need is for survival and security.

The 4 main attachment styles and their characteristics as a child, adult and a parent are:

- **Secure**: Safe, seen, comforted, valued, supported. This is the most common style.
    - **Child**: receives the nurturing and care needed, responds positively to contact and seeks comfort when frightened, may become upset when caregiver leaves
    - **Adult**: comfortable with intimacy and can balance dependence and independence in relationships, seeks emotional support from their partners and can provide the same in return
    - **Parents**: creates a compassionate environment, are capable of regulating their emotions, views their child as a separate person, but they also empathize with their child's experiences

- **Anxious**: One of the insecure attachment styles. This arises during childhood when parents are present and then suddenly absent, either physically or emotionally.
    - **Child**: experience distress when parent leaves and is difficult to sooth, are very sensitive and responsive to others's needs often at their own expense
    - **Adult**: tends to be codependent, has fear of abandonment and a need for validation, difficulty with setting boundaries, intense emotional discomfort and avoidance of being alone
    - **Parent**: over involve their child in their emotions and feelings, worry about and have high expectations of their parenting abilities

- **Avoidant**: Also an insecure attachment style. This occurs when a child is emotionally neglected.
    - **Child**: disregards affection from caregivers or shows aggression among other children
    - **Adult**: has shallow relationships, may be manipulative or abusive, suppresses emotions, strongly independent, trust issues, has extreme boundaries or is overly critical of themselves and others
    - **Parent**: can be strict and controlling, do not tolerate any strong display of emotion, disregards their child's attachment needs

- **Disorganized:** Also an insecure attachment style. This stems from intense fear, often as a result of childhood trauma, neglect or abuse.
    - **Child:** fearful, expresses ambivalent behavior towards parents, may distance or show aggression or freeze in parents presence
    - **Adult**: exhibits mixed feelings about close relationships, views themselves as unworthy of love, poor emotional regulation, low self esteem or being highly suspicious of other's intentions
    - **Parent**: struggles to build emotionally intimate relationship, behaves inconsistently or unpredictable

**Do you recognize your attachment style?** Are you a mix of more than one attachment style?

Understanding the different attachment styles will help you understand some of your characteristics and where they stem from.

"The root of suffering is attachment." - **The Buddha**

"Realizing what your attachment style is offers you a lot of freedom. It gives you a way to remember that at your core you are whole." - **Amanda Blair Hopkins**

"People have two needs: Attachment and authenticity. When authenticity threatens attachment, attachment trumps authenticity." - **Dr Gabor Mate**

## Me Again (Original poetry by Kelly Strand)

Years later
or has it only been a few
since I was just me
and I was with you

Time has passed
thinking I moved on
but finding myself
thinking of days gone

Remembering clearly
what I felt with you
trying to forget the
emotions I went through

The reasons I left
Were fulfilled by another
Only to find
I was left to wonder

Now that its just me again
Am I running to you
Or just running
To what I knew

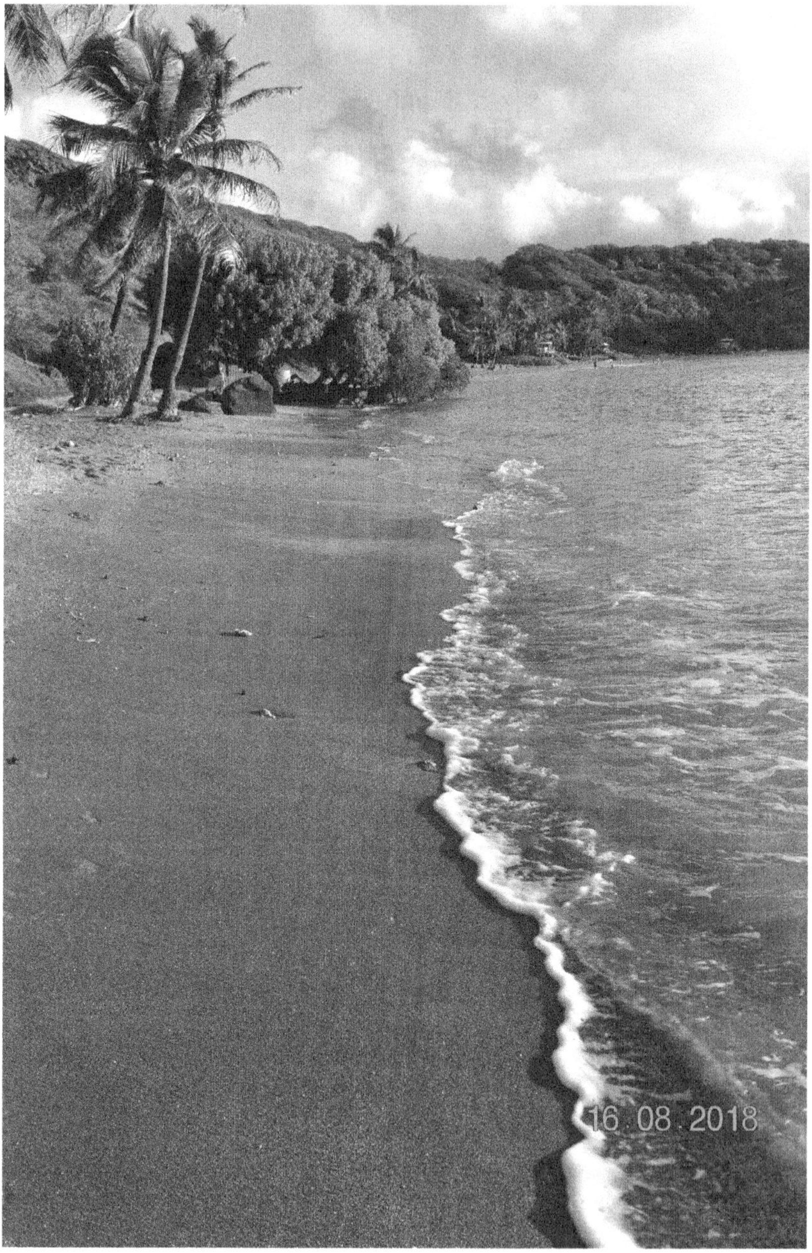
16.08.2018

# 6 IMPOSSIBLE = I'M POSSIBLE

Impossible = I'm Possible. Think about that.

**Impossible - definition**: not easy to deal with; not able to occur, exist or be done

**Possible - definition**: able to be done; within the power or capacity of someone or something.

You have the power. And whatever you put your mind to is possible. That includes your reactions to stressful events, the emotions you feel in response to everything in your life, and most importantly, how you choose to cope with your emotions.

**Emotion is energy** that exists in the body, ready to be triggered by external and internal stimulation. Emotions are energy in motion. When we try to block our emotions from flowing through our body they get stored in our organs, tissues, skin and muscles. They remain stored until we release them, and negative emotions have a long lasting effect on our body.

**Does this sound familiar?** Is this something that you do, and if so, where in your body does that emotional energy get stored?

It is very familiar for me. I blocked and bottled my emotions for so many years. Most of that emotional energy got stored in my shoulders and upper back. Whenever I would get a massage or someone would rub my shoulders they would comment that my muscles and tissue in that area were so tight.

I did a healing session one time with a Reiki and she could feel all of the stuck emotional energy in my upper back and shoulders. The emotions that were stuck in my upper back were sorrow and sadness, and the emotions that were stuck in my shoulders were due to burdens and responsibilities.

By recognizing how we cope with our emotions, and having the desire to change means that we are being intentional.

**Intentional - definition**: done on purpose; deliberate.

Are you being intentional in your life? **Intentional living** means taking actions and making decisions that are important to you and true to who you are.

Here are some principles of intentional living:

- **Own your authority.** Follow your instincts and have confidence in what you do and say.
- **Stay present.** Make an effort to stay in the moment in everything you do. Do not let your mind wander into the past or the future.
- **Follow the energy.** Recognize the energy around you in the the people you are with and the places you go. Stay with those where the energy feels good, and leave those where the energy does not feel good.
- **Use your intuition.** Learn to listen to your inner voice, and then trust it. Do not let your head get in the way.
- **Take care of yourself.** Make your self care your priority. Strive for wellness in mind, body and spirit.
- **Establish healthy boundaries.** Set your boundaries where needed. Accept them as healthy and necessary.
- **Release unwanted behaviors.** Admit and recognize the behavior. Identify the emotion behind the behavior. Watch for patterns and consciously do something different.

- **Emotional dexterity.** Hold the difficult emotions and thoughts loosely. Face them with courage and compassion and then move past them with your best self.
- **Surround yourself with beauty.** Find the beauty in everything around you. Be purposeful with things you allow in your space, and fill your space with things that make you feel good.
- **Honor your uniqueness.** Be proud of yourself and your unique qualities. Avoid comparison, and stop judging yourself. Accept your flaws, imperfections, strengths and talents. Pursue your passions and do not seek validation.
- **Be grateful.** Appreciate everything, every day. Say your gratitude prayers or keep a journal. Choose to focus your time and attention on what you appreciate.

**Are you living intentionally?** If not, what is standing in your way? Remember, the choice is yours.

"It's not about 'what can I accomplish?' but 'what do I want to accomplish?' Paradigm shift." - **Brene Brown**


"I'm not telling you it's going to be easy, I'm telling you it's going to be worth it." - **Art Williams**


"There is only one emotion, one energy, in the universe: the energy, the emotion, that we call love. When you know this everything changes." - **Neale Donald Walsch**

## Wandering Soul (Original poetry by Kelly Strand)

My thoughts have wandered
through the years
sometimes blinded
by the hurt and tears

Thoughts turn to questions
mostly unanswered
continually lingering
wanting to be heard

Am I not complete
what's missing from me
so many things I wish
I could clearly see

Sometimes clouded
By thoughts unclear
Often times stifled
By some inner fear

Happiness, I know only
Comes from within
Its time for my new
Life to begin

Coping On Your Journey

# 7 NEW STRATEGIES

We've talked a lot about some ways we cope and why. As mentioned before, coping is not a bad word, but it can become a dysfunctional crutch. As we focus on ridding ourselves of our maladaptive behaviors, let's explore some healthy ways of coping.

**The 4 A's.** The 4 A's are four ways in which you can handle stress or stressful situations in your life. The 4 A's should become your friends. When you find yourself in a stressful situation, pull the 4 A's out of your pocket and determine which of them you will choose to help you through it. The 4 A's are as follows:

- **Avoid** - Avoid unnecessary stress; people or situations that stress you out or cause you stress. Learn to say no.
- **Alter** - Alter the way you communicate. Try to think differently. Be willing to compromise. Express your feelings instead of keeping them inside.
- **Adapt** - Adapt different ways of proceeding. Adjust your standards. Reframe problems. Look at the big picture.
- **Accept** - Accept the things you cannot change. Do not try to control the uncontrollable. Focus on the positive.

Sometimes we find ourselves in a moment of panic and we need an immediate tool to help us. The **5-4-3-2-1 technique** is a grounding technique to help us in the moment, and is as follows:

Begin: Stop, close your eyes, take a deep breath in through your nose and out through your mouth, then -
- 5 - Open your eyes, look around and identify 5 things you can see. Say aloud what those 5 things are.
- 4 - Move your hands and identify 4 things you can feel. Say aloud the 4 things that you feel and describe how they feel.

- 3 - Close your eyes again, focus, and identify 3 things you can hear. Say aloud the 3 things you hear and the sound they are making.
- 2 - Breath deeply and identify 2 things you can smell. Say aloud the 2 things you smell and describe the scent.
- 1 - Move your tongue and identify 1 thing you taste. Say aloud the 1 thing you taste and describe it.

In my previous books I've mentioned some of the traits of Adult Children of Alcoholics/Dysfunctional Families and how growing up in a dysfunctional family causes children to cope in any way they can. Those coping skills follow children into adulthood and will stay there unless there is a conscious decision and commitment to unlearn those behaviors and adopt healthy ones.

My personal journey of healing from my childhood included learning about what it meant to be an adult child of an alcoholic (or other dysfunctional) parent. I invested the time to learn about the traits that defined me as I grew up, and how they were affecting me as an adult. There is a prescribed Spiritual 12 step program for Adult Children but I'm not going to go into detail about that. I will however, highly recommend it to you if you want to explore this type of spiritual program in your healing.

I do however, want to say that in addition to this program, and several years of personal therapy, I was able to meet some of the promises that are described as "The ACA Promises".

Some of the promises that I want to highlight are:

- Healthy boundaries and limits will become easy for us to set.
    - As I began to heal I became aware of the people in my life that I needed to have boundaries with. Learning that boundaries are healthy allowed me to define who, and to what extent, I would allow them in my life. With my youngest sister, I was able to tell her that I was setting a boundary and could not have her in my life due to the life choices she was making. I have set other boundaries for myself, which have allowed me to maintain relationships with people, but ensure that I do not absorb any of their negative energy.

- As we face our abandonment issues, we will be attracted by strengths and become more tolerant of weaknesses.
    - I had fear of abandonment issues that stemmed from inner child trauma. This led to me not having healthy relationships with men. I truly believed that if I loved someone then they would leave me, so I guarded my heart and never completely "loved" the men I chose to

have relationships with. I stayed in an unhappy relationship just so I was not alone. After 3 divorces and another long term relationship ended, I took a hiatus from dating and started therapy. I learned to understand my own weaknesses and work on them. I learned to understand my strengths and how they played together with my weaknesses. And as I started to heal, I was able to attract the right man into my life, and I was able to have a healthy relationship where we knew each other's strengths and weaknesses and embraced them together.

- We will choose to love people who can love and be responsible for themselves.
    - Loving someone should not involve trying to fix them. If you love them then accept them the way they are. Self love is the foundation of a person's happiness, and if you love someone who does not love themselves, they will never be completely happy with you or anyone else. I was in a relationship where I found myself trying too hard to "love" them and take care of them in order to make them happy. After my therapy, I realized that it is their responsibility to find their own happiness, and that I can only add to their happiness.

- Fears of failure and success will leave us, as we intuitively make healthier choices.
  - Having a fear of failure and a fear of success is difficult because every choice you make is weighed against those fears. You can't have success without failure, and the definition of success is different for everyone. The last few years I have taken some leaps of faith in my life, embraced my fears, and looked at everything as an experience instead of a success or a failure.

**Do you feel like you can start using some of these strategies?** I encourage you to pick one and try it for a month and then reflect on how it impacted you during the month.

"We have two strategies for coping; the way of avoidance or the way of attention." - **Marilyn Ferguson**

"Healing is not an overnight process. It is a daily cleansing of pain, it is a daily healing of your life." - **Leon Brown**

"When we can talk about our feelings, they become less overwhelming, less upsetting and less scary." - **Fred Rogers**

## **Unanswered Questions (Original poetry by Kelly Strand)**

Does time heal the wounds
Of a child inflicted by
A parent enslaved by a disease
And entrapped by a life of lies?

Can forgiveness take
Away the pain
And make a broken world
Be whole again?

If the reasons for sins
Were laid upon the table
Would weakness overcome
Or strength be able?

Would three wishes
From a bottled genie
Cause one to selfishly want
And be greedy?

What would foreseeing the answers
To those questions unanswered
Provide, or does
One really want to know?

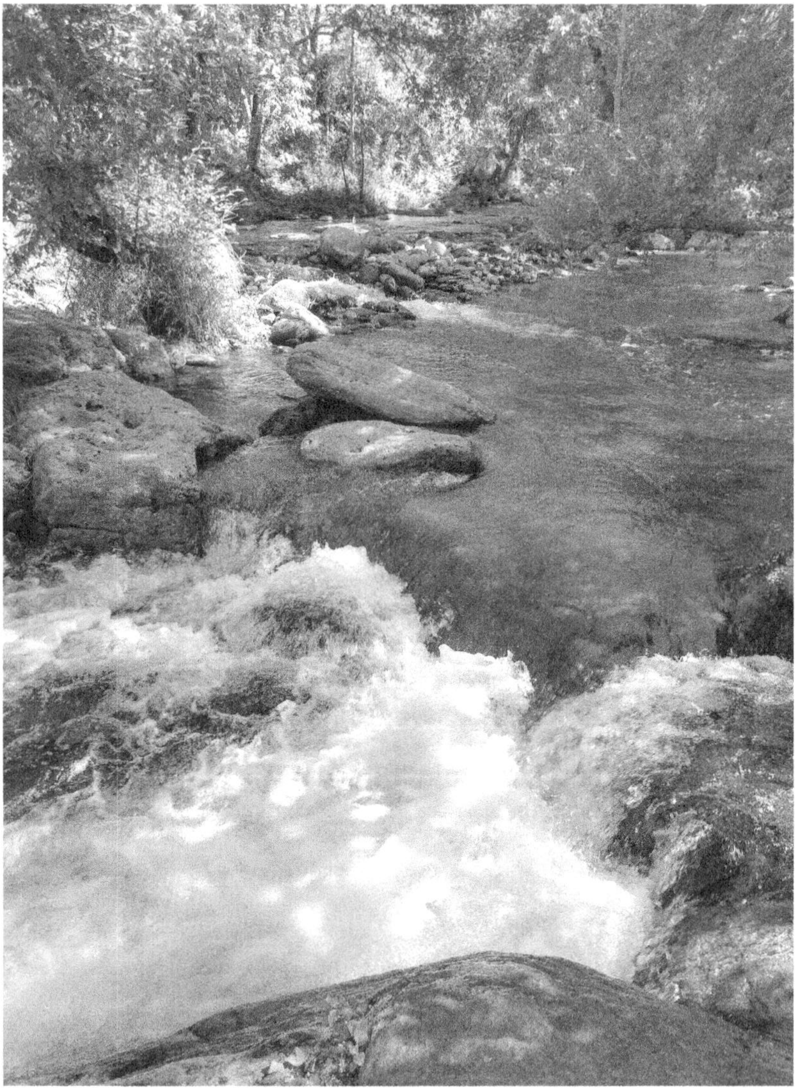

## 8 FIND YOUR CONTAINER

In one of my therapy sessions I went through an exercise of finding a container. A container is something that I can physically hold, open, and close. The purpose of my container is to hold my emotions. Any time I am struggling with my emotions or coping with a situation, I can pause, go get my container and put my emotions in the container. This can also be done metaphorically speaking, without actually having a container.

By putting my emotions in the container I can choose to leave them there, or go get them later when I am more mentally and emotionally ready to deal with them.

**Have you heard of, or ever had a container?** Does it sound kind of silly? I hope not.

The container is tool to help you cope. It's free. It can be anything you want it to be. And no one has to know about it. It's a "secret" container. **That sounds more intriguing doesn't it?**

My container is a small wooden box with sunflowers painted on it. It usually sits on my desk, but I move it around as needed.

Over the years I've had several things go into, and come out of my container. When I first started using my container it was kind of strange to get used to. Sometimes I would forget to put things in there. Other times, I was not quite sure how to open the container and take things out. But eventually I was able to get to a point where I recognized I was in a situation in which I needed to take a time out and go get my container. Then I was able to practice what I had been learning, and cope with the emotion that I had locked away in a calm, safe and controlled manner.

An example of the things that I choose to leave in the container are emotions that are resulting from triggers from my past. I am able to distinguish them now. I know that they are not "real" in the present situation, but they are leftover emotions from my past and represent parts of me that are not completely healed. By putting these emotions in my container, I am able to have clarity with the real emotions that I am experiencing in the present. These trigger emotions are emotions that I put in my container but do not retrieve. **Let me clarify that.** I do not retrieve them, but I do analyze them and determine that they are my trigger emotions, and since they are not real, there is nothing for me to do in order to process through them. So I consciously make the decision that they can stay there.

Some emotions do get retrieved though. An example of a time when I did retrieve my emotions from the box, was regarding an incident where someone lied to me and I caught them in the lie. The situation caused a flurry of emotions, and at that particular moment I was not able to calmly and clearly think about what I was feeling or make a decision on how I wanted to respond, so I put it in the box. I took the time I needed to digest the situation, take a step back and get myself grounded. Once I was ready I retrieved those emotions and processed them.

It is important to know how to use the container. It is not intended to be a one way container in which you only put things into it and do not take them back out. Consistently using the container will allow you to process your emotions in a healthy way.

"Unexpressed emotions will never die. They are buried alive and will come forth later in uglier ways." - **Sigmund Freud**

"Never rush an emotion; everything in life has a rhythm, it is the pauses and silences that speak the truth." - **Michael Jackson**

"It is not about managing your emotions; it is about managing your reactions to your emotions." - **Yung Pueblo**

**Letter to myself, written 7-31-18**

Dear Kelly,

I'm writing you to help you with your recovery. I'm learning things that are helping me cope and function normally and be in a healthy relationship. It's not easy.
I sill have strong instincts to run when I'm scared.
I'm learning it's ok to ask people for help, you're not alone. Being alone was a state of being that sheltered you from getting hurt and being disappointed.
I question myself a lot. My feelings and thoughts. What is real? Trust the process. It will take time, but it will work. You are recovering from almost a lifetime of dysfunction. You are making progress, so be easy on yourself. Put yourself first and only keep the promises to yourself.

Love you the most,
Kelly

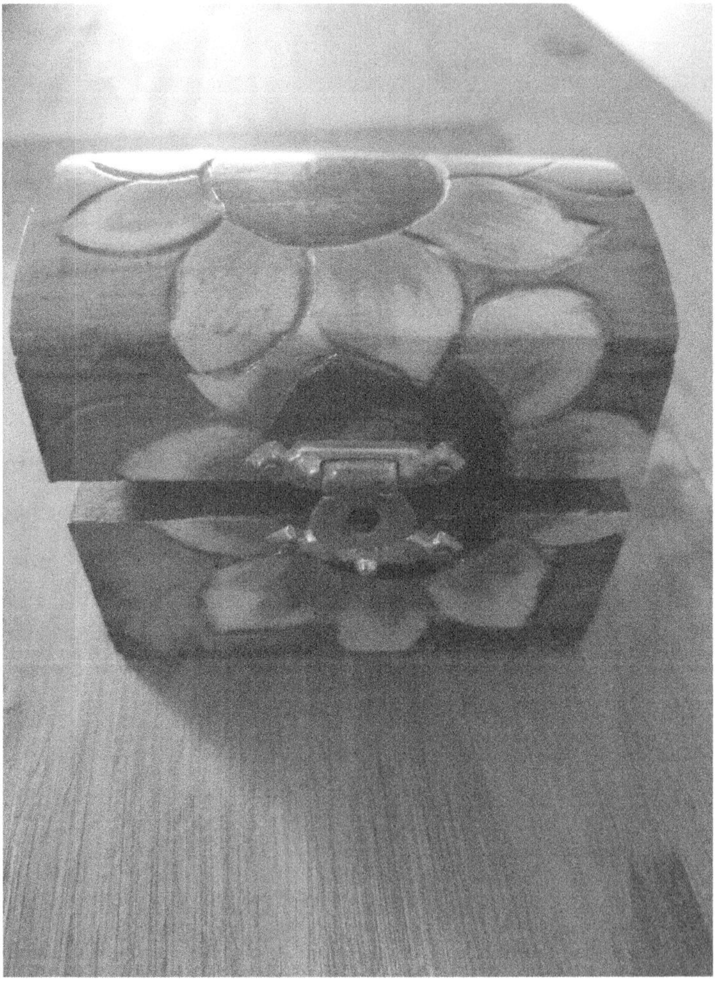

## 9 RESILIENCE

**Resilience. Definition:** the capacity to withstand, adapt, or to recover quickly from difficult or challenging life experiences and become stronger as a result; toughness

**Do you consider yourself resilient?** If not, why?

Have you ever known someone who always seems to bounce back quickly from adversity? Or maybe they seem tough enough to handle any situation? Those people are resilient. Do you want to be that person?

**Of course you do.**

No one goes through life without adversity, difficulties or challenges. Everyone has a choice in how they respond to adversity, difficulty and challenge. The choice is yours.
Sounds easy, right? Trust me, it's not so easy.
Deciding that you want to be more resilient, and embrace these new qualities is the first step. Resilience is your new friend, and there are some ways you can focus on strengthening your resilience.

I've mentioned before about the Wheel of Wellness, which encompasses our overall wellness in key areas of our life. We can also have a Resilience Wheel. This wheel includes key components to our personal resilience in life. We can practice examining the components of our Resilience Wheel and determine where we may need to focus our energy or ask for guidance or help to ensure each component is full and complete. The key components of the Resilience Wheel include:

- **Purpose** - our "reason why"; the bigger picture of our reason for being, or the goals we are working towards right now. Are you fulfilling your purpose or is it not on your to-do list yet?

"The biggest lie about purpose is that you find it. You don't find purpose, you choose it." - **Brant Menswar**

"If your path is difficult, it is because your purpose is bigger than you thought." - **Unknown**

- **Confidence** - the balance between the positive and negative thoughts and feelings about ourselves. Where is your self confidence on a scale of 1-10, and is it genuine?

"No one can make you feel inferior without your consent." - **Eleanor Roosevelt**

"Confidence is not "They will like me." Confidence is "I'll be fine if they don't." - **Christina Grimme**

- **Adaptability** - how we approach change and how we see change as an opportunity. Does change scare you or do you view it as an opportunity?

"Change is inevitable, growth is optional." - **John Maxwell**

"Embracing change is about adopting a growth mindset." - **Marco Marsans**

- **Support** - the people that we have in our life and how they contribute, either positively or negatively. What does your support circle look like and are they supporting you the right way?

"The right people will hear you. Even if you're not talking." - **Unknown**

"Anything is possible when you have the right people there to support you." - **Misty Copeland**

- **Meaning** - how we describe the events that happen to ourselves and others; the "stories" of our lives. Are your stories like the black and white daily newspaper or like a full color encyclopedia?

"Life is not merely a series of meaningless accidents or coincidences, but rather it is a tapestry of acts that culminate in an exquisite, sublime plan." - **Serendipity**

"Life is a handful of short stories, pretending to be a novel." - **Unknown**

- **Energy** - how energized or de-energized we are thinking or feeling about what's happening in or lives and what we need to achieve. Is your energy level sufficiently charged, and what are you attracting with it?

"Every thought has a frequency. Thoughts send out a magnetic energy." - **Rhonda Byrne**

"No one can create negativity or stress within you. Only you can do that by virtue of how you process your world."
- **Wayne Dyer**


The quotes above are pretty powerful and inspiring words. If you feel like you need to fill your Resilience cup up a little, then I challenge you to make your Resilience wheel and focus on it for a month and see what positive changes transpire in your life.

## Troubled Soul (Original poetry by Kelly Strand)

When your path
Is paved
Keep your eyes
Ahead

Do not
Look back
Or
Question

Struggling with what you
Know and
What you know
Is right

Do not sway
Resist the urge
To turnback
To a rocky past

Coping On Your Journey

## 10 CLOSING

I hope, that after reading this book, you are able to look at the ways in which you are coping in your life and have a better understanding.

There are healthy and unhealthy ways of coping, and unfortunately when you grow up with dysfunction you usually end up learning unhealthy coping skills.

You are in control now, and the choice is yours. You have already taken the first step in recovery by sharing in my journey.

I have shared some specific, but easy to use techniques and strategies that can help you adapt the ways in which you cope. By understanding your past, and finding the courage to face your uncomfortable emotions, you are taking the steps needed.

## Passing Through (Original poetry by Kelly Strand

From beginning to end
in all that we do
our life has a purpose but
we are just passing through

Is our destiny certain
or do we have some control
on which way our predetermined
life path will go

We are mind body and spirit
with all we are whole
human in form
They each play a role

Our mind is our engine
That controls our being
Houses memories and
Gives everything meaning

Our body gives us form
Unique from each other
We only have one
In this lifetime together

Care must be given to
Nourish cleanse and feed
Body mind and soul on our journey
As we're just passing through

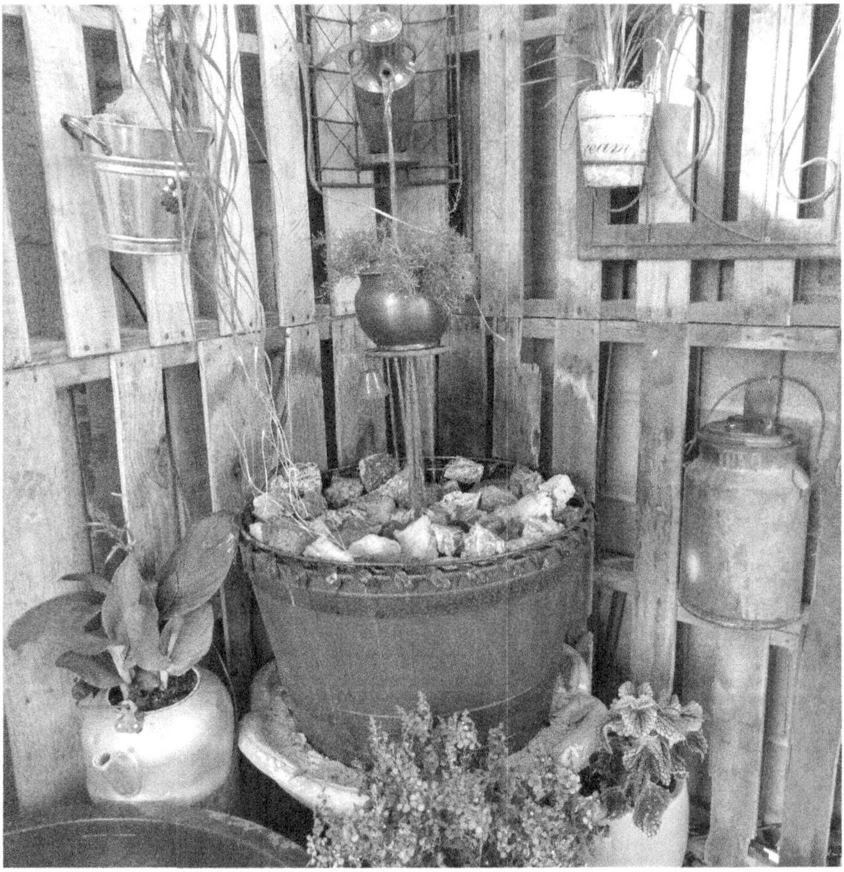

## ABOUT THE AUTHOR

Kelly currently lives with her partner Erik in Arizona, part time in Tonto Basin and part time in Fountain Hills.

In Tonto Basin they have a ranch where they are living sustainably, growing their own food, raising a large flock of chickens and other birds and producing natural skincare and CBD products.

In Fountain Hills she focuses on her writing and coaching and they focus on growing their wellness business.

She is blessed with an amazing daughter who is independent, strong and beautiful inside and out; a son who who is free spirited, easy going and currently serving in the Navy; and she is a very proud Grandmother to two grandchildren.

She focuses on staying balanced in mind/body/spirit with a holistic approach to health and wellness and is living her best life.

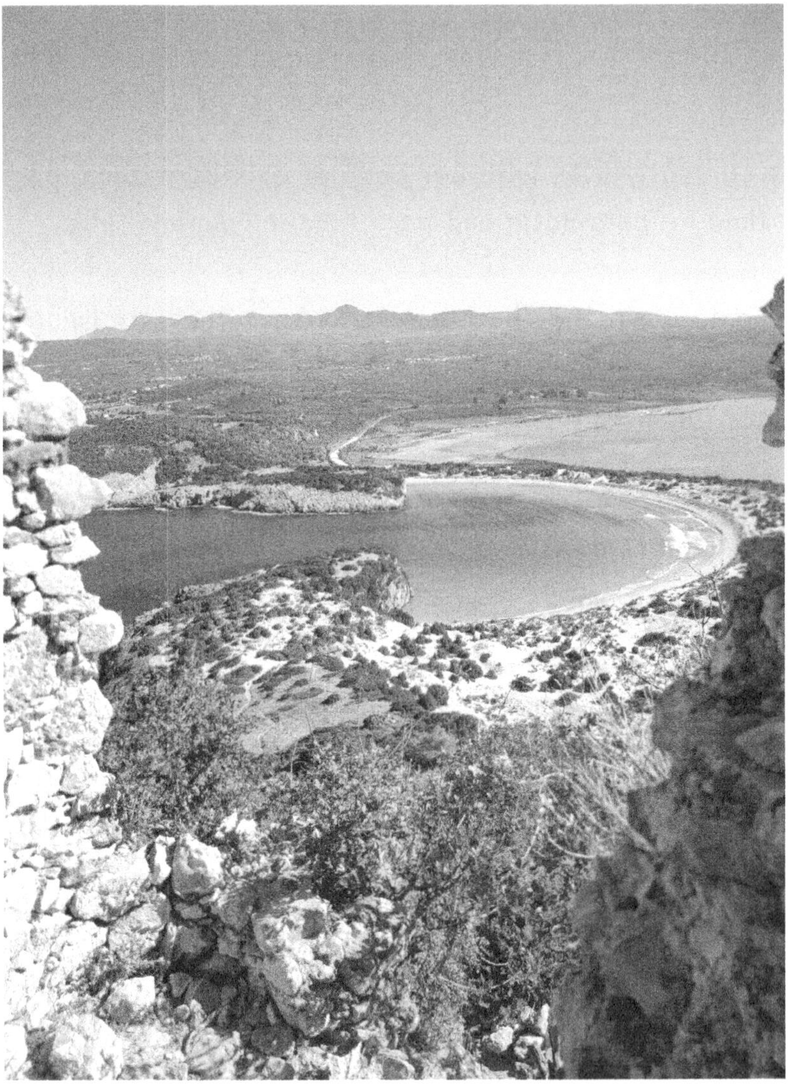

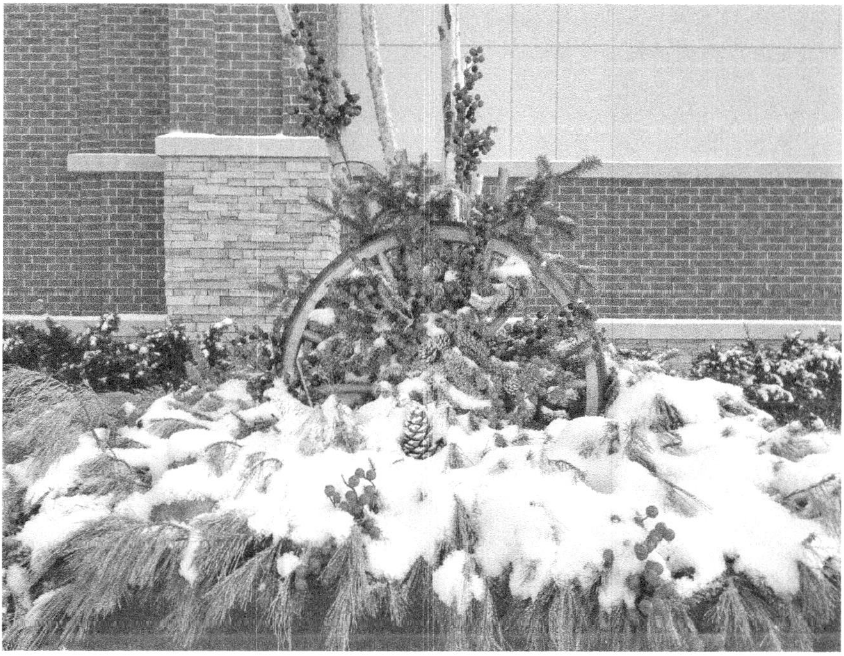

…

Made in the USA
Las Vegas, NV
30 July 2023